PLANNING PROSPERITY : A BEGINNER'S GUIDE TO INVESTING, ASSET CLASSES AND PERFORMANCE ANALYSIS

DIBAKAR BALA

Made with ♥ on the Notion Press Platform
www.notionpress.com

Contents

CHAPTER ONE

The Importance of Investing

Why should anyone invest their money? This is a question that many people ask, especially those who are new to the world of personal finance and investing. The answer is simple: investing is a crucial step towards achieving financial security and building wealth for the future.

There are several reasons why investing is important. First, it allows you to take advantage of the power of compound interest, which is the concept that the interest earned on an investment is added to the principal, and the resulting total is then used to calculate the interest in the next period. This means that over time, the value of your investment will grow exponentially, allowing you to earn more and more money without having to put in any additional effort.

Another reason why investing is important is that it can help to protect you against inflation. Inflation is the general increase in the prices of goods and services over time, and it can erode the purchasing power of your money if you do not take steps to protect yourself. By investing your money, you can earn returns that are higher than the rate of inflation, which means that your money will retain its purchasing power and you will be able to maintain your standard of living in the future.

Investing can also help you to diversify your portfolio, which is the practice of spreading your investments across different asset classes in order to reduce risk. By diversifying your portfolio, you can protect yourself against losses in any one particular asset class and increase your chances of achieving your financial goals.

In addition to the benefits mentioned above, investing can also provide you with a sense of control and empowerment over your financial future. By taking an active role in managing your money and making informed investment decisions, you can take control of your financial situation and work towards achieving your long-term goals.

In conclusion, investing is an essential part of achieving financial security and building wealth for the future. It allows you to take advantage of the power of compound interest, protect yourself against inflation, diversify your portfolio, and take control of your financial situation. Whether you are just starting out on your financial journey or you are an experienced investor, it is never too late to start investing and taking control of your financial future.

CHAPTER TWO

Where to Invest Your Money

Now that you understand the importance of investing, you may be wondering where to invest your money. There are many different options available to investors, and the right choice will depend on your individual financial goals and risk tolerance.

One option is to invest in stocks, which are ownership shares in a company. By investing in stocks, you can potentially earn a higher return on your investment than you would with other types of investments, but there is also a higher level of risk involved. Stocks can be volatile, meaning their prices can fluctuate greatly over time, and there is no guarantee that you will earn a profit on your investment.

Another option is to invest in bonds, which are loans that are made to governments or corporations. When you invest in bonds, you are essentially lending your money to the issuer in exchange for regular interest payments and the eventual return of your principal. Bonds are generally considered to be less risky than stocks, but they also typically offer lower returns.

Another option is to invest in mutual funds, which are investment vehicles that pool the money of many investors and invest in a diversified portfolio of stocks, bonds, and other securities. Mutual funds can offer a higher level of diversification than individual stocks or bonds, and they can be a good option for investors who want to invest in a variety of assets but do not have the time or expertise to manage their own portfolios.

Finally, you may want to consider investing in real estate, either by purchasing a property and renting it out or by investing in real estate investment trusts (REITs), which are companies that own and manage a portfolio of real estate assets. Real estate can offer a steady stream of income and the potential for long-term capital appreciation, but it also carries its own unique risks and requires a significant amount of capital to get started.

In conclusion, there are many different options for where to invest your money, and the right choice will depend on your individual financial goals and risk tolerance. It is important to do your research and carefully consider your options before making any investment decisions.

CHAPTER THREE

Things to Know Before Investing

Before you start investing your money, it is important to understand some key concepts and considerations that will help you make informed decisions and maximize your chances of success.

First, it is important to understand the different types of investments and the risks and potential returns associated with each one. As mentioned in the previous chapter, some common investment options include stocks, bonds, mutual funds, and real estate. Each of these asset classes has its own unique characteristics and risks, and it is important to understand these before you invest.

Next, it is crucial to have a clear understanding of your financial goals and how investing can help you achieve them. Whether you are saving for retirement, building an emergency fund, or trying to grow your wealth, it is important to have a plan in place and to choose investments that are in line with your goals.

Another important consideration is your risk tolerance, which is your willingness and ability to accept the potential for losses in exchange for the possibility of higher returns. Your risk tolerance will play a major role in determining the types of investments that are right for you, and it is important to be honest with yourself about your risk tolerance in order to avoid making investments that are too risky for your comfort level.

It is also important to understand the fees and costs associated with investing, as these can have a significant impact on your returns over time. Different investments have different fees and costs, and it is important to be aware of these before you invest.

Finally, it is crucial to do your research and make informed investment decisions. This means reading up on different investment options, seeking the advice of financial professionals, and staying up-to-date on the latest developments in the world of investing. By taking the time to educate yourself and make informed decisions, you can increase your chances of success and achieve your financial goals.

In conclusion, there are several key things to know before investing your money. It is important to understand the different types of investments, have a clear understanding of your financial goals, be aware of your risk tolerance, understand the fees and costs associated with investing, and do your research and make informed decisions. By taking these steps, you can increase your chances of success and achieve your financial goals.

CHAPTER FOUR

What is the Stock Market?

The stock market is a marketplace where stocks, which are ownership shares in a company, are bought and sold. When you invest in the stock market, you are essentially buying ownership in a company and becoming a shareholder.

The stock market operates on the principle of supply and demand, meaning that the price of a stock is determined by the balance between the number of people who want to buy the stock and the number of people who want to sell it. When there is high demand for a stock, its price will typically increase, and when there is low demand, its price will typically decrease.

The stock market is a key component of the global financial system, and it plays a vital role in facilitating the flow of capital between investors and companies. By providing a platform for buying and selling stocks, the stock market allows companies to raise capital from investors, and it allows investors to earn returns on their investments.

The stock market is also a key indicator of the overall health of the economy. When the stock market is performing well, it typically indicates that the economy is strong and that investors are confident in the future prospects of the companies they are investing in. Conversely, when the stock market is performing poorly, it can be a sign of economic weakness and investor uncertainty.

In conclusion, the stock market is a marketplace where stocks are bought and sold, and it plays a vital role in facilitating the flow of capital between investors and companies. It is an important indicator of the overall health of the economy and can provide investors with the opportunity to earn returns on their investments.

CHAPTER FIVE

What are IPOs?

An initial public offering (IPO) is the process by which a privately-held company becomes a publicly-traded company by issuing shares of its stock to the public for the first time. When a company goes public through an IPO, it is offering its stock for sale to the general public, and this can be an attractive opportunity for investors who are looking to buy into a company at an early stage of its growth.

There are several reasons why a company might choose to go public through an IPO. One reason is to raise capital, which is money that the company can use to fund its operations, expand its business, or pay off debt. By offering its stock for sale to the public, a company can raise a significant amount of money that can be used to support its growth.

Another reason why a company might go public through an IPO is to increase its visibility and credibility. When a company goes public, it is subject to a higher level of scrutiny from regulators, investors, and the general public, and this can help to enhance its reputation and credibility.

Finally, going public through an IPO can provide liquidity for the company's existing shareholders, meaning that they can sell their shares on the stock market if they choose to do so. This can be particularly attractive for investors who have been involved with the company from an early stage and are looking for an opportunity to cash out some or all of their investment.

In conclusion, an IPO is the process by which a privately-held company becomes a publicly-traded company by issuing shares of its stock to the public for the first time. This can be a valuable opportunity for investors who are looking to buy into a company at an early stage of its growth, and it can provide significant benefits for the company itself, including the ability to raise capital, enhance its reputation, and provide liquidity for existing shareholders.

CHAPTER SIX

Absolute Returns vs. CAGR vs. XIRR

When it comes to evaluating the performance of an investment, there are several different metrics that can be used. Two common metrics are absolute returns and compound annual growth rate (CAGR), and a third metric that is often used in the context of investments with irregular cash flows is the extended internal rate of return (XIRR).

Absolute returns measure the total return on an investment over a specific period of time, expressed as a percentage of the initial investment. For example, if you invest $100 and your investment grows to $120 over the course of a year, your absolute return would be 20%. Absolute returns can be useful for comparing the performance of different investments, but they do not take into account the time value of money, meaning that they do not adjust for the fact that money is worth more in the present than in the future.

CAGR, on the other hand, does take the time value of money into account. It is a measure of the average annual rate of return on an investment over a specific period of time, assuming that the investment compounds at a steady rate. For example, if you invest $100 and your investment grows to $120 over the course of a year, your CAGR would be 10% (assuming a one-year investment period). CAGR is useful for comparing the performance of investments with different time horizons, but it can be misleading if an investment's returns are not consistently compounded over time.

XIRR is similar to CAGR, but it is specifically designed for investments with irregular cash flows. For example, if you invest a lump sum of money and then make additional investments or withdrawals at different points in time, XIRR can be used to calculate the average annual rate of return on your investment over the entire investment period. XIRR is useful for evaluating the performance of investments with irregular cash flows, such as those made through a mutual fund or a real estate investment trust (REIT).

In conclusion, absolute returns, CAGR, and XIRR are all useful metrics for evaluating the performance of an investment, but they each have their own strengths and limitations. Absolute returns measure the total return on an investment over a specific period of time, but they do not take the time value of money into account. CAGR takes the time value of money into account, but it can be misleading for investments with non-consistently compounded returns. XIRR is specifically designed for investments with irregular cash flows, but it is not suitable for investments with consistent cash flows.

CHAPTER SEVEN

The Power of Compounding

Compounding is the process by which the returns on an investment are reinvested, resulting in the growth of the initial investment over time. For example, if you invest $100 and earn a 10% return in the first year, you will have $110 at the end of the year. If you then reinvest the $10 in returns and earn another 10% return in the second year, you will have $121 at the end of the second year. The $11 in returns from the second year are then reinvested, and the process continues, resulting in exponential growth over time.

The power of compounding is the phenomenon by which the returns on an investment grow exponentially over time, thanks to the reinvestment of returns. This is a key concept in the world of investing, and it is the reason why the earlier you start investing, the more time you have for your investment to grow and compound.

For example, if you start investing $100 per month at the age of 25 and earn an annual return of 10%, by the time you reach the age of 65, you will have accumulated over $1 million in savings. However, if you wait until the age of 35 to start investing, you will have accumulated just over

$400,000 by the time you reach the age of 65, even though you are investing the same amount of money each month. The earlier you start investing, the more time you have for your investment to grow and compound, and the more you can benefit from the power of compounding.

In conclusion, compounding is the process by which the returns on an investment are reinvested, resulting in exponential growth over time. The power of compounding is the phenomenon by which this growth occurs, and it is a key concept in the world of investing. The earlier you start investing, the more time you have for your investment to grow and compound, and the more you can benefit from the power of compounding.

CHAPTER EIGHT

Growth vs. Value Investing

Growth and value investing are two different approaches to investing in the stock market. Growth investors are typically focused on companies with strong potential for future growth, while value investors are typically focused on companies that are undervalued relative to their intrinsic value. Both approaches can be successful, but they have some key differences that investors should be aware of.

Growth investors are typically looking for companies that have the potential to grow at a faster rate than the overall market. They are willing to pay a higher price for a company's stock in the expectation that the company will deliver strong future growth. Growth investors are typically focused on metrics such as revenue growth, earnings growth, and the potential for new products or markets.

Value investors, on the other hand, are focused on companies that are undervalued relative to their intrinsic value. They are looking for companies that are trading at a lower price than what they believe the company is worth. Value investors typically use metrics such as price-to-earnings ratio, price-to-book ratio, and dividend yield to identify undervalued companies.

One key difference between growth and value investing is the potential for short-term volatility. Growth stocks can be more volatile in the short term because their future growth prospects are less certain, and investors are willing to pay a higher price for the potential for future growth. Value stocks, on the other hand, can be less volatile in the short term because they are trading at a lower price relative to their intrinsic value, and investors may be more willing to hold onto them even if the market is volatile.

Another key difference is the potential for long-term performance. Growth stocks have the potential to deliver strong long-term returns if they are able to deliver on their growth potential. However, if a growth stock fails to deliver on its growth prospects, it can underperform the market and result in losses for investors. Value stocks, on the other hand, may not have the same potential for strong long-term returns, but they can provide a margin of safety against potential losses because they are trading at a lower price relative to their intrinsic value.

In conclusion, growth and value investing are two different approaches to investing in the stock market. Growth investors are focused on companies with strong potential for future growth, while value investors are focused on companies that are undervalued relative to their intrinsic value. Both approaches can be successful, but they have some key differences, including the potential for short-term volatility and long-term performance. Growth stocks can be more volatile in the short term, but they have the potential for strong long-term returns if they are able to deliver on their growth prospects. Value stocks may not have the same potential for strong long-term returns, but they can provide a margin of safety against potential losses.

Ultimately, the best approach for any individual investor will depend on their investment goals, risk tolerance, and personal preferences.

CHAPTER NINE

Alternative Investments

Alternative investments are financial assets that do not fit into the traditional categories of stocks, bonds, and cash. They can include a wide range of assets, such as real estate, commodities, hedge funds, private equity, and derivatives.

One key characteristic of alternative investments is that they are often less liquid than traditional investments. This means that it can be more difficult and time-consuming to sell alternative investments and convert them into cash. This can be a disadvantage for investors who need quick access to their money, but it can also be an advantage for investors who are willing to hold onto their investments for a longer period of time.

Another key characteristic of alternative investments is that they can offer investors the potential for higher returns, but they also carry a higher level of risk. For example, real estate investments can be subject to market fluctuations and changes in property values, while commodities such as gold and oil can be affected by changes in supply and demand. Hedge funds and private equity can be particularly risky because they often employ complex investment strategies and can be highly leveraged, meaning that they use borrowed money to amplify their returns.

Despite the risks associated with alternative investments, they can play an important role in a well-diversified investment portfolio. By including a mix of traditional and alternative investments, investors can potentially reduce their overall portfolio risk and improve their potential for long-term returns. For example, real estate investments can provide a hedge against inflation and offer a stable source of income in the form of rental payments. Commodities such as gold and oil can provide a hedge against economic downturns and geopolitical risks. Hedge funds and private equity can offer the potential for higher returns, but they should only be considered by investors with a high risk tolerance and a long-term investment horizon.

In conclusion, alternative investments are financial assets that do not fit into the traditional categories of stocks, bonds, and cash. They can include a wide range of assets, such as real estate, commodities, hedge funds, private equity, and derivatives. Alternative investments can offer investors the potential for higher returns, but they also carry a higher level of risk. Despite the risks, alternative investments can play an important role in a well-diversified investment portfolio by providing a hedge against inflation, economic downturns, and geopolitical risks.

CHAPTER TEN

Bonds, Debentures, and NCDs

Bonds, debentures, and NCDs are all types of debt securities that are issued by companies and governments to raise capital. They are popular investments for both individual and institutional investors, and they can provide a stable source of income in the form of periodic interest payments.

Bonds are debt securities that are issued by governments and companies to raise capital. They typically have a fixed term, and the issuer agrees to pay the bondholder a fixed rate of interest over the life of the bond. At the end of the term, the issuer also agrees to repay the principal amount of the bond to the bondholder.

Debentures are a type of long-term debt that is issued by companies to raise capital. They are similar to bonds in that they offer a fixed rate of interest and a fixed term, but they are unsecured, meaning that they are not backed by any specific assets of the issuer.

NCDs, or non-convertible debentures, are a type of debenture that cannot be converted into equity shares of the issuer. They offer a higher interest rate than regular debentures, but they also carry a higher level of risk because they are unsecured and the issuer has no obligation to convert them into equity.

One key difference between bonds, debentures, and NCDs is the level of risk. Government bonds are considered to be the least risky because they are backed by the full faith and credit of the issuing government. Corporate bonds and debentures are considered to be more risky because they are not backed by any specific assets and are subject to the creditworthiness of the issuer. NCDs are considered to be the most risky because they are unsecured and offer a higher interest rate, which can be attractive to investors but can also increase the risk of default.

Another key difference is the potential for returns. Government bonds typically offer a lower interest rate than corporate bonds and debentures because they are considered to be less risky. Corporate bonds and debentures can offer a higher interest rate, but they also carry a higher level of risk. NCDs can offer the highest interest rate, but they also carry the highest level of risk.

In conclusion, bonds, debentures, and NCDs are all types of debt securities that are issued by companies and governments to raise capital. They offer a fixed rate of interest and a fixed term, and they can provide a stable source of income for investors. However, they also carry varying levels of risk, depending on the issuer and the specific type of security. Investors should carefully consider the risks and potential returns of these investments before deciding whether they are suitable for their investment portfolio.

CHAPTER ELEVEN

Conclusion

In this book, we have explored a wide range of topics related to personal finance and investing. We have discussed the importance of having a financial plan, the different types of investment vehicles, the role of risk and return, and the various investment strategies that can be used to achieve financial goals.

We have also covered the basics of financial planning, including budgeting, savings, and debt management. We have discussed the importance of setting financial goals, and we have outlined the steps that can be taken to develop a personalized financial plan.

In addition, we have examined the different types of investment vehicles, such as stocks, bonds, mutual funds, and real estate, and we have discussed the risks and potential returns of each. We have also explored alternative investments, such as commodities, hedge funds, and private equity, and we have discussed the role they can play in a well-diversified investment portfolio.

Throughout the book, we have emphasized the importance of understanding the risks and potential returns of different investment options, and we have provided guidance on how to develop an investment strategy that is tailored to individual financial goals and risk tolerance.

In conclusion, personal finance and investing are complex and dynamic fields that require knowledge, discipline, and patience. By following the principles outlined in this book, and by seeking professional advice when necessary, individuals can take control of their financial lives and work towards achieving their financial goals.

Creating A Better Investment Portfolio

As an alumnus of IIT Kharagpur and a former quant researcher at a multinational hedge fund, I have a deep understanding of the financial markets and investment strategies. In this final chapter, I would like to share some tips on how readers can use the knowledge and techniques discussed in this book to create a better investment portfolio.

First, it is important to have a clear understanding of your financial goals and risk tolerance. This will help you determine the appropriate asset allocation for your investment portfolio, and it will also guide you in selecting the specific investment vehicles that are most suitable for your needs.

Next, you should consider diversifying your investment portfolio across a range of asset classes, such as stocks, bonds, mutual funds, and real estate. This will help to reduce your overall portfolio risk, and it will also provide the potential for higher returns over the long term.

In addition, you should consider including alternative investments in your portfolio, such as commodities, hedge funds, and private equity. These investments can provide a hedge against inflation, economic downturns, and geopolitical risks, and they can also offer the potential for higher returns. However, they are also riskier and less liquid than traditional investments, so they should only be considered by investors with a high-risk tolerance and a long-term investment horizon.

Another important factor to consider is the use of investment strategies, such as dollar-cost averaging, rebalancing, and tax-loss harvesting. These techniques can help you manage your portfolio more effectively and potentially improve your long-term returns.

Finally, it is important to monitor your investment portfolio regularly and make adjustments as needed. This may involve rebalancing your portfolio to maintain your desired asset allocation, selling underperforming investments, and buying new investments that align with your financial goals and risk tolerance.

In conclusion, creating a better investment portfolio requires a combination of knowledge, discipline, and patience. By following the tips and strategies outlined in this book, and by seeking professional advice when necessary, you can take control of your financial future and work towards achieving your financial goals.

Printed by Libri Plureos GmbH in Hamburg,
Germany

9 798889 092179